Easy eCourse Profits

How to Make Money Selling What you Know Online Using Three Simple Web Tools

Chris Lutz

DEDICATION

I dedicate this book to all of the other authors and mentors that have allowed me to learn this knowledge and lifestyle.

Table of Contents

ACKNOWLEDGMENTS

I'd like to acknowledge all those working hard to make a living online. Keep up the good work. Persistence is key. You're doing the right things and those who are persistent will be successful.

Introduction: Why eCourses?

Having paid products to offer your customers is a key part of any online business. Traditionally, these have come in the form of eBooks – digital books that can be downloaded and read at leisure.

However, if you're trying to teach something, the eBook isn't always the most popular format. This is where eCourses come in – they are simply digital versions of courses that will deliver information and training in bite-sized, step-by-step chunks.

eCourses are easy to send out because they can be delivered directly via email. And getting into your customer's inbox makes it much more likely that your information will be read!

eCourses have traditionally been seen as an excellent freebie – an incentive to get people to sign up to your mailing list. But eCourses can be products in their own right, and extremely profitable ones at that!

Going Beyond Standard Information Products

When you are trying to think of ways to make more money in your business it's likely that the idea of having a membership website has come up. The volume of money to be made is unlimited, and it comes in month after month. However, the sheer volume of work to do to get that started stops you.

You'd have to build a secure website with a message board, and a learning center, and then you'd have to monitor it constantly. You don't have that much knowledge of technology so someone quoted you a hefty price tag to build it for you. Money you don't have. The cost of entry into the membership market it just too high.

But, what if I told you that you could make membership volumes of money without having a membership site. Instead, you can create paid eCourses that are delivered automatically to the person who has paid for them. Your only job is to create the eCourse which amounts to writing some articles, loading them into your email list software like Aweber, and setting up a Pay Now button with PayPal? Would you be interested then?

Aweber + PayPal = Dollars

Offering paid eCourses to your audience is truly a lot less hassle than other membership or subscription models. They're an excellent choice if you're limited on time, if you don't want to deal with the techy side of memberships, or if you simply want to work smarter.

All you'll need is two key ingredients: a payment processor and an autoresponder service. It's likely you already have these, but if not, we recommend Aweber and PayPal.

PayPal: Unless you want to write free eCourses, you're going to need a way for people to send you money to sign up. PayPal is, without a doubt, the top payment processor. Nearly everyone has used it before, and your customers will trust it. You can either create one-time payment buttons, or recurring subscription payments. We'll show you how to do this.

Aweber: Aweber is an email marketing service that makes it easy for your customers to subscribe to your mailing lists (you can have as many mailing lists and you'd like). You can then set up a sequence of emails to be delivered at an interval you set. You might think you can do this all yourself on your computer, but using an email marketing provider means it's all 100% automated.

What Will This Cost?

If you're worried about the cost of these two services, don't be! PayPal charges a small fee per transaction, and Aweber starts at just $19 per month (with a 1 month trial for $1). That's far cheaper than setting up complicated membership software, or hiring people to do everything manually!

How Much Money Can You Make?

Think about it: If you built a 12-week course you could charge as little as $20 a week and if you get 10 people to sign up you'll be making $200 a week. That's $200 dollars per week! This is additional revenue that you simply set up and forget about.

If you set up the course right, and market right you're likely to get more than 10 members in any given week. If you write and compile a compelling eCourse it's likely that most of your members will stick with it through the 12 weeks, and there will always be new sign ups because you don't have to start it over. It all runs automatically and you can have any number of people on lesson 1 while some are on lesson 5.

You don't have to have a ton of technical knowledge to start an eCourse membership or subscription. If you currently know how to use your WordPress website, Aweber, and PayPal you can have a membership site set up within a couple of hours. This is what this guide is all about. No fuss, no muss.

Are you ready?

Why eCourses = More Money With Less Hassle

If you're not yet convinced about the beauty of the eCourse then here are a few reasons that might help:

1) No Technical Knowledge Needed

Email eCourses are very easy to set up compared to paid products and memberships. Whether you do a free

T. (New Document)
◄ ► untitled text 12 ⬍
1   If you know how to type, you're
2   half way to creating an eCourse ;)

eCourse or a paid eCourse the steps are pretty much the same. You probably already have a newsletter using email software like Aweber, and you can simply keep using this for your eCourse.

You'll write your eCourse in your favorite text editor, then load up your emails by cutting and pasting them into Aweber. You'll create a PayPal pay button, and the "thank you" page will be the sign up form via Aweber. Your members will sign up, and the delivery of the eCourse is on autopilot!

(Confused by that? Don't worry – we cover it all step by step later on!)

2) No Need to Converse With Your Students

When you're running an eCourse, you don't have to ever even talk to your students. Of course, if someone has a problem you may need to deal with some customer service issues - you can let your virtual assistant handle that if something comes up. But since the member is in charge of unsubscribing via PayPal and you'll ensure that this information is available on every single email you send out, there is very likely never going to be any reason to communicate with your students yourself other than within email. Simple!

3) Earn Residual Money for Working Once

An eCourse has the potential to keep earning money years after you have created it. This is called residual income. It's the kind of income where you work once, but keep getting paid well into the future.

How does that work? Well, once you set everything up into your email service (like Aweber) and have the PayPal subscription button on your site, everyone who signs up now and in the future will start at the beginning of the eCourse. As long as you keep your email service and website online, people can sign up for years to come.

4) You Can't Start Making Money Right Away

You don't have to complete your entire eCourse before you start selling it, meaning you can bring that money in fast!

Here's an example – you plan on selling an eCourse that's 12 weeks long before it ends. However, you've only written the first week, so you start selling it right away. You then make sure you write and load each new lesson one week at a time until it's complete. Your customers will never even know it wasn't complete at the time you launched! And, once you're done with all 12 weeks, you're done, for good. Yet, you'll still be bringing in money (see point 3 above).

5) You Don't Even Have to Write It

Finally, you don't even have to write the eCourse yourself! An eCourse is the perfect place to compile and use private label rights (PLR). This kind of content is cheaper to buy than unique, ghostwritten content since it's sold to multiple buyers. You can break up any "how to" eBook or report to create a fabulous eCourse that you can make your own and promote.

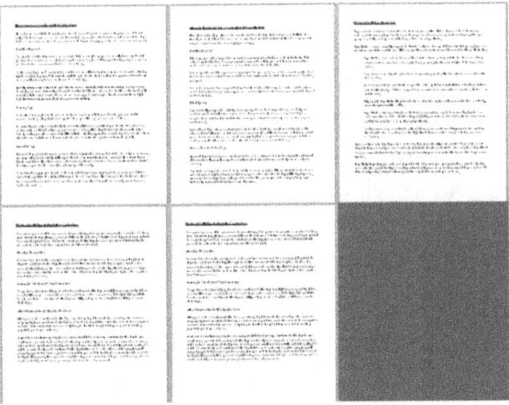

Just add in some of your own words and make sure the advice is up-to-date, especially if it has to do with technology, and you're done. You can even outsource this entire process to your virtual assistant. Then you can sit back and collect the money.

Are eCourses A Business Model In Themselves?

The great thing about eCourses is that the entire idea can be used as your complete business model. You can simply create a lot of different eCourses for various niches, market them through various sales pages, and make your money just doing that.

Or, you can use eCourses as an addition to your current product funnel. Your eCourse could be one step away from getting customers to sign up to a webinar, teleseminar or other in person event. Or it could be a couple of steps away from one-on-one coaching with you.

In other words, your eCourse can be an end in itself (i.e. profit making business model), or it can be a way to get people used to buying lower-cost products for you before selling higher-ticket programs and services.

eCourses as a Business

If you decide to make eCourses your main business, you can choose more than one niche, create a

small website or sales page, Facebook community, Twitter handle, and so on for each niche that you're involved with. Then, using only one Aweber account, you can set up many different eCourse subscriptions.

Once you create each eCourse then you only need to spend time and money marketing the eCourse. If you set up an affiliate program, all the better. The types of eCourses you can set up are truly unlimited. Only your imagination can stop you.

eCourses as Part of Your Product Funnel

The more likely way that you'll involve yourself with paid eCourses (and maybe even free ones) is making them an addition to your current product funnel.

A free eCourse could be at the widest part of your funnel to get people to sign up for your newsletter. In that case, you can take more liberties with each section of the course and market your other products and services along with the course content.

If you create a paid eCourse, it can be at a smaller point in your product funnel, at a lower price. Afterwards, you might then promote a webinar, or teleseminar and then go on to promote one-on-one coaching. eCourses are a great way to give your audience a taste of your in person offerings.

Earning Residual Income is The Goal

Plus, the very top of your product funnel before one-on-one anything it's always a great idea to seek **residual income**.

Residual income is the only way to make regular money without more work. Residual income means that you worked once and you're making money over and over again without working again (save for smaller maintenance and customer service tasks).

Of course, you will have to continually market your eCourse, but if you set up an affiliate program some of that marketing will also be on autopilot. If you don't have an affiliate program starting one is not difficult or very technical if you use a good program.

Whether you decide to make it your business to create eCourses for a variety of niches or just one, or whether you make an eCourse part of your current product funnel is up to you. And it's perfectly natural for your goals to change over time. Whatever you do, though, you must take action!

6 Steps to Easily Create Unlimited eCourse Ideas For Any Niche

You may be sold on the idea of eCourses as a great moneymaker, but you're afraid. You don't know if you can actually create an eCourse or not. You don't even have a clue what to teach so even if you were to outsource the job, you can't even provide an outline at this point!

Well, there are ways to cut through all that self-doubt and negative self-talk.

1) Use Mind Maps

A mind map is a great way to overcome any type of inability to develop new ideas. You start with a clean sheet of paper, write the main topic (your niche) in a circle in the middle of the paper. Let go of all judgment and start writing different aspects of your niche down. Make a line from the center, to subtopics, then lines from subtopics to even smaller topics all related to the center circle that is your niche.

Want to do all this on your computer instead of by hand? Try downloading FreeMind – it works on both Mac and Windows.

Tip:

You can find mind maps about almost anything already on the net. Do a search for your niche and "mind map".

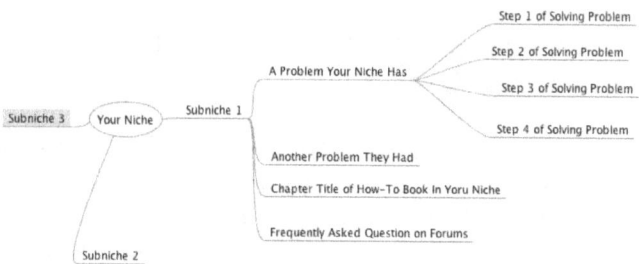

2) Focus on the Fear

The next thing you need to do in order to come up with good eCourses is to focus on the fear in your mind map. Within the mind map are going to be some frustrations that your niche will have that you need to find solutions for. If you can come up with a solution to any problem you can create an eCourse about it.

Think in terms of "how to" do anything. How to write better. How to learn better. How to cook better. It's all very simplistic right now, but you want to find one main idea on which you can create a course.

You can also look to a few useful online sources to discover what the top fears are in your niche:

- Look at what people regularly discuss in forums,
- Search for questions about your niche on Yahoo Answers,
- Put yourself in your reader's shoes. What do they care most about? What holds them back? What frustrates them?

Open Question   Show me another »

How to lose weight in a month?

ish

Hi, I am a 19yr old male, I weight about 180 and my height is 5'7. My doctor said that
was too much for my height and that I had to lose weight. I am still hound so I know I
can lose a lot within a month. I haven't exercise in a while now, so everything I do
gets me tiered very fast. What are some ways I can exercise without getting tired
quickly .... Btw I have asthma but not very serious only when I do heavy exercise
......

1 hour ago - 4 days left to answer.   ⚐ Report Abuse

Answer Question

3) Ditch the Doubt

Right now your negative self-talk is at an all time
high. You're wondering why you should be the one
doing this. Who are you to teach anyone anything?
Well, the fact is, you are the right person to teach
anything that you already know about, or are willing
to learn about.

Teaching can be daunting, but while you're
having doubts, why not write down all your doubts
and make them into positives. That's right, if you
doubt that you're the right person for this course,
you can improve your situation by learning more
about the subject. If you hate how your course
looks, make it better. Just don't stop.

4) Take From Others

Most teachers actually get their initial ideas from
others, then they add in their own personality to the
mix. You can do that as well, even in an eCourse.
No, don't plagiarize, but you can read tables of
contents in "how to" books to come up with ideas
for you to use. It's even okay to use someone else's
book to teach a course, that's exactly what
teachers do. You simply point your students in the
right direction, with select quotes and suggestions

for further reading.

5) Break it Down

Once you have an idea of what you want to teach, break it down into small steps. It might help you to actually go through whatever it is that you're teaching, taking notes along the way so that you don't miss any important steps. Name each step something creative that gets your student's attention, then focus on the minutia of each step. Don't leave anything out.

For instance, if you're telling them how to bake bread, you don't want to leave out a lesson about the difference between all purpose flour and self-rising flour. You're teaching someone how to do something that they have no idea about, so don't leave out any information or step no matter how minor.

6) Build in Interaction

To make your course even better, you can, if you want to, build in some type of interaction such as sending a survey to your students mid course to find out what they've learned so far. This will help you create even better courses. All of this can be automated so while it will feel interactive to them, you won't have to do anything but set it up, make a thank you letter, and send it out. The students' actions trigger the next automatic response from your autoresponder.

How to Write Your First eCourse

Okay, don't be scared, eCourses are fast and easy to set up. I promise!

As humans we tend to make things a lot more complicated than they really are. Instead, we should seek to work smarter, instead of working harder. **eCourses are the answer to working smart**.

You only have to create the course (or have it created) then put it into your email list service like Aweber, set up one sales page in which you include a PayPal button.

Here's how to go about creating the course content. We'll cover the setup in a later section.

The DIY Route

There are a lot of different ways that you can get your course created. The cheapest way is to create the course yourself. If you want to go this route then here's what to do:

Step 1: The Basics

You've already brainstormed ideas earlier on, but now it's time to put them together in a coherent course format. First things first, you need to decide how long you want your course to last for. It could be 6 weeks, it could be 6 months, it could be a year! It really depends how much you have to say and what you're teaching.

Step 2: Outline

Now that you know how long your course is going to be, break it down into the correct number of steps. For example, if it's a 6 month course and you'll be emailing out every week, break it down into 26 steps.

Note down briefly what you'll cover in each step. Once you've done that, have a look again and make sure everything flows in logical order. If not, jiggle things around until they're just right.

Step 3: Research

Some people like to research ahead of time, to save time on the writing stage. If there are certain facts and figures you need to know, note them down now. Also keep a note of different resources you find that'll help you with each section on your outline.

Step 4: Write!

Now that you've got your outline, writing should be easy! And don't be too daunted by the fact that you've got a whole course to write – remember, you can start selling the course after the first part is written. You can then simply complete the next stages from week to week.

Outsourcing Your eCourse

Writing isn't for everyone! Whether you struggle to get things out in a coherent way, or you just don't have time, you can also outsource. You could even complete the outline, as mentioned above, and give this to someone to "fill in the blanks".

You can find people to outsource to through your own network by asking colleagues who they use. Or you can use job sites like Upwork and Elance.com to find the perfect person to help you create a fabulous eCourse.

It's up to you how you proceed. Outsourcing is an easy way to get your course done fast. Just be sure that you have a clear idea of what you want created before you place your advertisement. That way the professionals that bid on your project understand what is expected of them, and when you choose one, you'll know that you've done your best to explain what you want.

Using Content Shortcuts

Another way to create an eCourse is to repurpose content that's already been written.

For example, if you're a blogger then you might

already have a lot of content written on a certain subject. You can take blog posts you've already written, combine them and add to them to create a complete eCourse.

Or perhaps you've already released eBooks and reports in the past, whether free or paid, and you want to develop the subject into a course. Simply break them down into single topic sections, cut and paste into the Aweber system as follow up messages. Add an intro and conclusion, maybe ask the student to do some task, and that's it.

Simply create a schedule for them such as one per week on a specific day if you like. Each person who signs up will be on a different schedule but will get their lessons one per week like everyone else. If someone drops out, they'd have to start over with the first lesson. It's good to let them know that in your introduction email.

Remember:

Creating an eCourse is so simple, it's not any harder than creating your normal broadcasts or scheduled email for newsletter subscribers. If you can do that, you can do this!

How You Can Use Video & Audio in Your eCourse

Now that you understand how to create a text based eCourse, did you know that you can make your courses even more sticky and exciting by adding video to the mix? Well, you can, and it's not any harder than adding text.

Note that adding video and audio has a number of benefits.

- Firstly, it satisfies different kinds of learners. Some people prefer to read, while others learn better by watching or listening. Including all elements will help people absorb your information better.

- Secondly, video and audio increases the perceived value of your eCourse, meaning you can charge more for it!

How to Add Video & Audio to Your eCourse

If you're using Aweber, it offers an easy way to send video messages via email. Even if you're using a different email service that doesn't let you embed video, you can simply link to a page on your website containing the video. Simply describe the video to your student, then send them to a page to view the video.

You can also house videos in a number of other places too including YouTube via unlisted videos. You can also store your videos on Amazon S3 Cloud Storage. It's simple to use and the cost is minimal. It's a great way to add additional interest to your eCourse.

What Should You Record?

Videos are a really great way to get technical "how to" information to your students. You don't need to have every lesson as a video, but including a couple in your over all course is a great idea.

You can use screen capture software like Camtasia to create awesome video training. Making demonstration videos is a great way to impart tricky or confusing step-by-step instructions to your students. Plus, they'll enjoy hearing your voice explain how to do things to them. They will feel closer to you and more trusting of you once they view a video even if they never see your face.

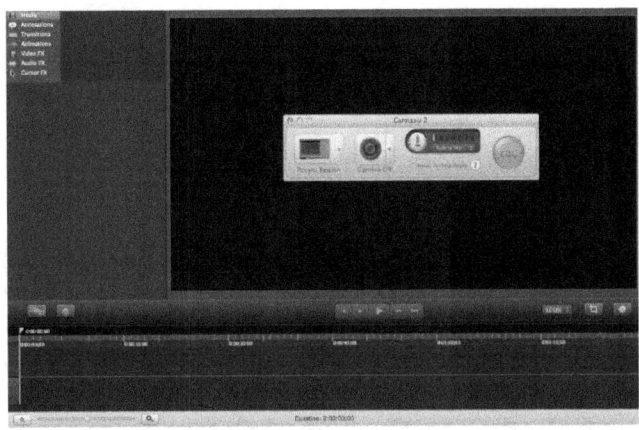

In fact, it doesn't even have to be your voice, or you creating the videos. You can absolutely outsource this, just like you can the entire eCourse development.

A great idea for including video in your eCourse is to include a video introduction. It's a nice way to make face-to-face contact with your students in a way that doesn't require you to do it over and over again. Just create a nice welcome video, include everything you would as text, and your students will enjoy watching it. It's nice to give the choice of watching the video or reading the text since some people might not be in an area where they can easily listen to voice.

If you've ever had a webinar on any aspects of your course you can simply include that webinar recording as one of the lessons in your eCourse. It's a great way to repurpose content that you've created in the past to use in your eCourse.

If you've ever conducted an interview or given

an interview about any of the topics in your eCourse it is a nice addition to include the audio with a relevant lesson. Any time you can make use of content that you've already created, whether it's a blog post, a video, a podcast, an eBook or something else, all the better.

Your students will enjoy being connected to you in that way and it will help disseminate the information you're trying to impart in more than one way, which increases the stickiness of the lesson. The more your students remember and apply what they've learned, the more likely they are to trust you with other eCourses and information.

Tip:

It is recommended that you also provide a transcript if you're going to include video or audio in your eCourses.

Step By Step eCourse Setup

You've done all the hard work, now it's time to set everything up. Remember, this isn't hard! It's a lot easier than setting up a membership site, and we've listed each step here. If you need more help, make sure to refer to the accompanying worksheets.

1) Create a Sales Page

A sales page is a page where you place your eCourse for sale, and where people can click through to buy it via PayPal. It's really just another page to your website. You can create a dedicated webpage with its own URL for each of your courses, or you can use your current domain name and add a new page.

Your sales page should explain the pain points that you can solve with your eCourse and how your eCourse is different and the answer and ideal solution to their problems. Save this page as a draft.

2) Create a PayPal Button

Go into PayPal and create button. There are two types of button you might use: a subscription button if you want recurring payments (e.g. every week or month), or a one-time payment button. Set it up to charge your members however you want to charge them. Remember what you called this button.

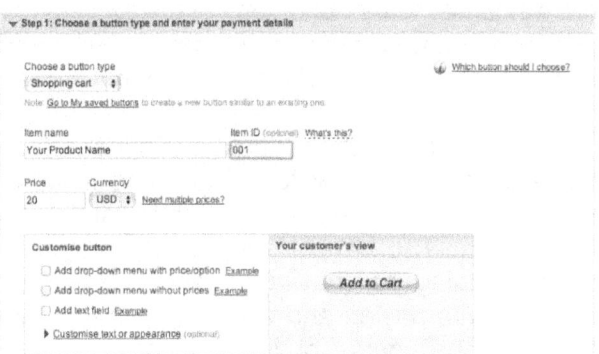

3) Set up Aweber

Go to Aweber and set up a new list. It's under "Create and Manage Lists". Ideally, you'll name this new list after your eCourse. Remember what you call this list.

4) Link Your List and Your Payment Button

Now load up the Aweber PayPal app here: https://www.aweber.com/users/apps

If you've never used it before, you'll need to follow some initial set up instructions. Once you've done that, you can link the button you just created with the list you just created.

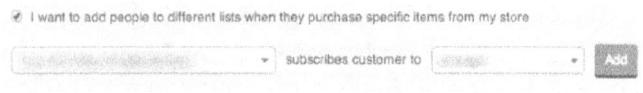

5) Load eCourse into Aweber

Go ahead and load each section of your course into Aweber. Start with a thank you for subscribing, or welcome letter and an overview letter that describes exactly what the student will be learning over the course of the X weeks or month.

Your welcome letter should explain exactly what the student gets, how to contact you if there are problems with delivery, how to white list your email address, how to cancel and unsubscribe and the risks of doing so (having to start all over), how much they're paying and when and what to expect. Including the course outline and a syllabus is an excellent way to get your audience excited.

6) Test!

Now all you need to do is edit and review each page that you've created and then make all the pages live. Then you need to find someone to test out the system to be sure every step works and is understandable. You can refund their money for testing it. Tell them you'll refund their money after the 2nd week (alternatively you can pay them up front for a couple of weeks) and allow them to keep getting the course for free in exchange for testing it out for you.

How to Price Your eCourse

One of the hardest and most important things to do in any business is to choose a price point.

You must somehow come up with a price point for every eCourse you want to sell to your audience. Conversely, you might have good reason to offer the eCourse for free - such as wanting to make money through recommendations, a future longer eCourse or other products and services.

The way in which you come up with a price point is part science, part art, and part a big fat guess!

The Value Perception You Create

Your target audience has a certain value perception about you that you've created over time. You create this value perception with the content of your blog posts, your emails and your social media interaction. You even create your value perception through the products you recommend and use yourself. You're constantly creating your audience's value perception about you even when you don't realize it. Even the design of your website or blog sends a message of value to your audience.

How Many People Want What You Have?

Another factor in pricing is how many people want what you have. This can affect your pricing of an eCourse both up and down. After all, there is value in volume selling, which can help lower a price. But, there is also value in selling something for a higher price in order to eliminate some of the audience. Especially if the point of the eCourse is to introduce them to an even higher priced event later such as one-on-one coaching. If you want the most possible students taking your eCourse because you want to create a larger audience of fans, then you'll price it lower.

Your Target Audience's Ability to Pay

It's very important that you know who exactly your audience is, and what they can afford. If you price yourself out of your target audience's ability to pay you will see a low volume of sales. If you price too low for your audience the value of the eCourse will go down in their eyes and they might not sign up for it based on the low price, which they perceive as low quality. Know your target audience inside and out. You should have created an ideal client persona by now, given them a name, a job, an income, so that you can what they want, need and can justify buying.

What Your Competition Charges

A really good way to get an idea into what you should price your eCourse at is to look at what your competition is charging for a similar product. It won't hurt you to actually purchase the product so that you can see what's in it. How does your compare? Can you make improvements to yours so that yours is better and charge more? Is your product already a lot better? By evaluating what your competitors are charging you can get closer to your right price. You may want to charge a little less or more than your competition depending on how you want your products to be perceived.

What Your Audience Wants to Pay

You can survey your audience and let them tell you exactly what they'd pay for your eCourse. Let them vote on a few different price points, then go with the one that the most voted for. It might be shocking that they usually don't pick the lowest price point. But, even if they do, you are picking price points for them to choose from that you are happy with. Test out different price points for your eCourse. Which one gets the most traction? Stick with that price point.

How to Make More Money From Every eCourse You Create

Once you've finished your eCourse, don't think that the earning potential stops there. A really great thing about eCourses is that you can even make money from free eCourses!

There is ample opportunity to earn money through an eCourse that you might not have thought about. Here are just a few ideas to maximize your eCourse profits.

Affiliate Product Recommendations

Option 1:

Throughout your eCourse you're likely going to need to recommend certain tools or paid services to your customers. For example, in this guide you're reading right now, we recommend you sign up to Aweber for the delivery of your eCourses.

As long as you truly recommend these products and services, it's perfectly fine to use affiliate links throughout your eCourse. If you really want them to implement your course it's important that you not shy away from sharing. This means you'll get extra money when your customers sign up as a result of your recommendation.

Don't go overboard on this, however – you don't want to put people off by making them feel as though you're only there to sell to them! Do not use banner ads or give them the hard sell. Instead just slip the affiliate links within the text of your email, or as a P.S. under your signature.

Option 2:

If you aren't interested in worrying about any tech issues then you'll simply deliver all your weekly/ monthly lessons via email autoresponder. However, if you're willing to put *slightly* more work in then each email lesson can link to a <u>download page</u>.

The download page simply has a list of links to the PDF versions of the current lesson for download, plus all previous lessons the student has already downloaded. It's really easy to set up a download page.

Tip: Give the page a name that no one can guess (to prevent unauthorized access to your content).

Aside from that, you can add a few additional money making items:

- You can use banner ads on the download page, which are related in some way to your eCourse. Perhaps your students will need certain software to do what you're teaching them. Maybe your students need a special ingredient that is hard to find. Whatever it is, you can link to it on the download page and earn more money.

- You can also use the download page as a way to communicate more information to your students then add a P.S. - "here are some of the tools I use".

- What's more, since this is another page on your website, they'll see the menu items and after downloading their lesson they can easily click through to look at your other offerings.

Lead Into Other Products

Don't just promote affiliate products in your eCourse – don't forget that you also want to be leading into more of your own products (if you have them).

Maybe you offer one-on-one coaching? If so, be sure to remind students that, if they need more help at the end of their eCourse, they can sign up.

Or maybe you've got eBooks or other eCourses on related topics? Don't forget to promote them at the end of your eCourse or at any point where they might be applicable!

Repurpose Your eCourse

Once your eCourse is written you can just leave it as it is. That's perfectly fine, and the beauty of the eCourse means that you can still make money from it for many years to come.

However, it's also possible to re-use and re-purpose the eCourse into something more. Here are a few ideas…

- You could re-purpose the eCourse into an in-person training event,
- You could use the eCourse as the basis for paid one-on-one coaching,
- You can take the content as the eCourse and turn them into a webinar,
- You can create a more detailed book based on your eCourse,
- You can take a free eCourse, add to it and eventually sell it as a paid course,
- You can give the eCourse away as a bonus to a larger paid product you produce in the future.

Get creative with your thinking and you'll see that there are multiple ways to earn more from that eCourse you put out there!

10 Ways to Market Your eCourse

Once you've written everything and loaded all your content ready to go, it's time to market your eCourse! Well, actually, during your creative process it's time to market your eCourse. Yes, start marketing right

away by creating little hints in your communications with your audience. People will get more excited about it if you tease them.

Here are 10 ways to make more sales of your eCourse and keep that recurring revenue coming in:

1) Create a Killer Sales Page: The first thing people will see about your eCourse is likely your sales page. Ensure that you've created a couple of sales pages in which to test. Go all out with the sales page giving your potential student all the information they need to make the choice to sign up for your eCourse. Use appropriate imagery that helps them envision the benefits of taking your eCourse. Make your call to action very clear and obvious.

2) Create Social Buzz: Tease your social media audience by discussing what you're creating. Talk about how excited you are to be working on this fabulous new eCourse and how you know it's going to help so many people. The more you talk about it before it's launched the better, but keep mentioning it after it's out there too.

3) Blog About It: As you are in the creation process you also want to blog about the various parts of your eCourse. Whet the appetite of your audience by giving sneak peeks into what the course will entail. Make them excited about launch day by promising some additional bonuses for students.

Once it's already launched, use blog posts to give snippets of lessons without giving everything away. You can also blog about related topics, making sure to link to the sales page for your eCourse each time you do.

4) Guest Blog About It: Try to submit guest posts about your topic to various authority websites in order to build up links back to your website. If your eCourse isn't live yet, create a space holder sales page for people to sign up to receive the announcement via email when the course is done. The link should be the exact same link that will house the real sales page. That way, once launched people who click though to your page via your bio will go directly to the sales page.

5) Do Interviews: Find places such as blogtalkradio.com that speaks to your niche to do interviews with. Create a profile that explains who you are and what you do and why you're a great person to interview and send it out to various bloggers and movers and shakers within your industry. More than likely they'll love to interview you if you present yourself well.

6) Get Reviews & Testimonials: Allow a select few to preview a few lessons of your course in exchange for an honest review that you will use on your sales page, in all marketing materials and on social media. You can offer them a link back to their  website in exchange for the review. If you can get someone who is very popular to vouch for your eCourse you'll attract a lot more buyers.

7) Announce First to Your List: Give your email list first dibs on the eCourse. Give them a special price just for being on your email list and part of your audience already. This is also a good way to get testimonials. Ensure that within your eCourse that you always ask for testimonials from satisfied students. This can be accomplished by including a simple link to a Google Form near the end of the eCourse.

8) Host a Free Webinar: This works very well if you can get some others to host the webinar with you. Each of you will be using the webinar to market something that you offer, for you it will be the eCourse. Ensure that you all offer complementary products and services to the same audience and aren't too much of direct competition. The more hosts you can involve the larger your audience will be.

9) Get Your Affiliates Excited: Create terrific sales material for your affiliates. They will need graphics in various sizes and colors, as well as pre-written emails, blog posts and more that they can edit and make their own. Other ways to encourage them including holding an affiliate contest with prizes for certain sales milestones, or giving affiliates a higher cut of what they sell for a limited time.

10) Send Out a Press Release: Finally, don't forget to send out a press release about your eCourse. The fact that you've created a helpful eCourse is a newsworthy event in your business and should be announced in all ways possible. Press releases still work, and you might find yourself getting more local audience members by sending the press release locally too.

By using all of these methods to market your eCourse you're sure to turn out a successful eCourse that will add to your bottom line today, tomorrow and far into the future.

Finding Your Way Around PayPal

How to Create PayPal Buy Buttons

Lutz

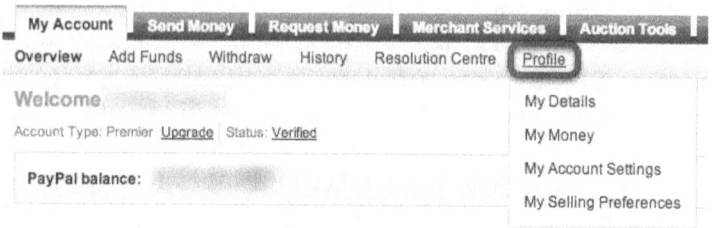

First, login to your PayPal account. Then click **Profile.**

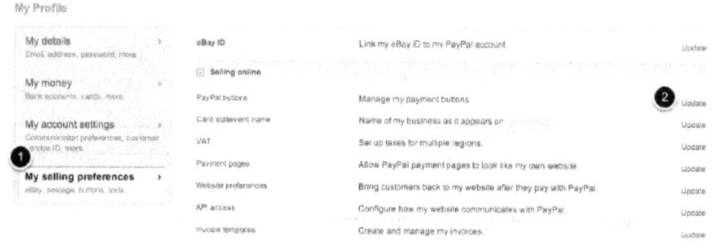

Now, click **My Selling Preferences**, and then **Update** next to **PayPal Buttons.**

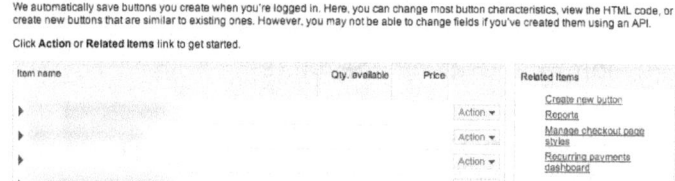

Now you'll be shown a list of previous buttons you've created, in case you want to edit them. Or you can create new buttons from this page by clicking **Create New Button**.

Option 1: Creating a One Time Payment Button

If you only want your customer to pay one time for your product - so that they won't be billed in future - then you need to create a standard payment button. First, click **Create New Button** on the page you were just on.

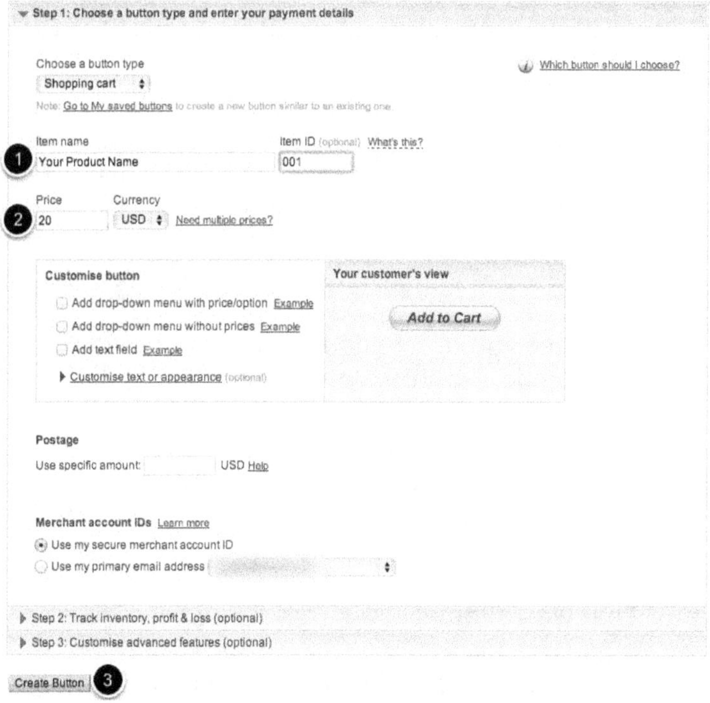

▼ Step 1: Choose a button type and enter your payment details

Choose a button type   ⓘ Which button should I choose?

Shopping cart ▾

Note: Go to My saved buttons to create a new button similar to an existing one.

Item name   Item ID (optional) What's this?

① Your Product Name   001

Price   Currency

② 20   USD ▾ Need multiple prices?

Customise button   **Your customer's view**

☐ Add drop-down menu with price/option Example

☐ Add drop-down menu without prices Example   **Add to Cart**

☐ Add text field Example

▶ Customise text or appearance (optional)

Postage

Use specific amount: USD Help

Merchant account IDs Learn more

◉ Use my secure merchant account ID

○ Use my primary email address (   ) ▾

▶ Step 2: Track inventory, profit & loss (optional)

▶ Step 3: Customise advanced features (optional)

Create Button ③

39

Next, fill in the options. This is super simple and there are very few required fields. However, take a look at the advanced options in case you have more specific requirements.

You'll probably only need to enter an item name, a price, and then click **Create Button.**

Add your button code to your webpage

You just created customised HTML code for your button. The final step is to copy the code from this page and paste it into your website editor.

Copy the button code:

1. Click **Select Code**.
2. Right-click and copy the selected code.

If you're working with a website developer, you can paste the button code into an email and send it to your developer now.

Paste the button code in your website editor:

The code must be pasted in the "code" view, where you can view and edit HTML.

1. In your website editor or admin page, open the page where you want to add your button.
2. Look for an option to view or edit HTML.
3. Find the section of the page where you want your button to appear.
4. Right-click and paste your button code into the HTML.
5. Save and publish the page. (The preview function in your editor may not display the button code correctly.)
6. Test the button to make sure it links to a PayPal payment page.

Need more help? Click here for additional information.

Website Email

```
<form target="paypal" action="https://www.paypal.com/cgi-bin/webscr"
method="post">
<input type="hidden" name="cmd" value="_s-xclick">
<input type="hidden" name="hosted_button_id"
value="5M7HKQH28MK54">
<input type="image"
src="https://www.paypalobjects.com/en_GB/i/btn/btn_cart_LG.gif"
border="0" name="submit" alt="PayPal – The safer, easier way to pay
```

Buyer's View

Add to Cart

Select Code   Go back to edit this button

Once you've created your button, you'll get some code like this. You can use the HTML code on your website, and the email code in emails. Just follow the instructions PayPal gives for using your links. You can then link this into your Aweber eCourse by using Aweber's PayPal app (see the separate tutorial).

That was simple!

Option 2: Create a Recurring Payment Button

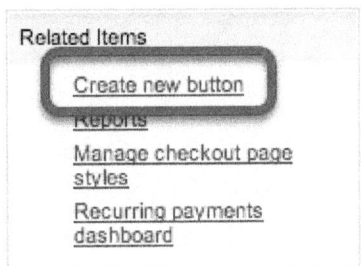

If you want your customers to pay more than once - for example they pay every month to get continued access to your course - then it's similar to what you just did. There are just a few changes. First, like before, click **Create New Button** from the saved buttons page in your PayPal account.

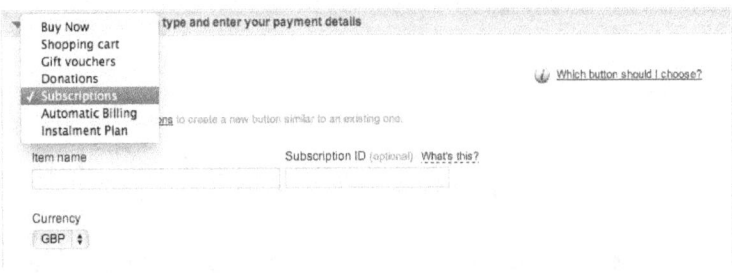

Next, you need to fill in the options again, except this time you need to select **Subscriptions** from the dropdown menu.

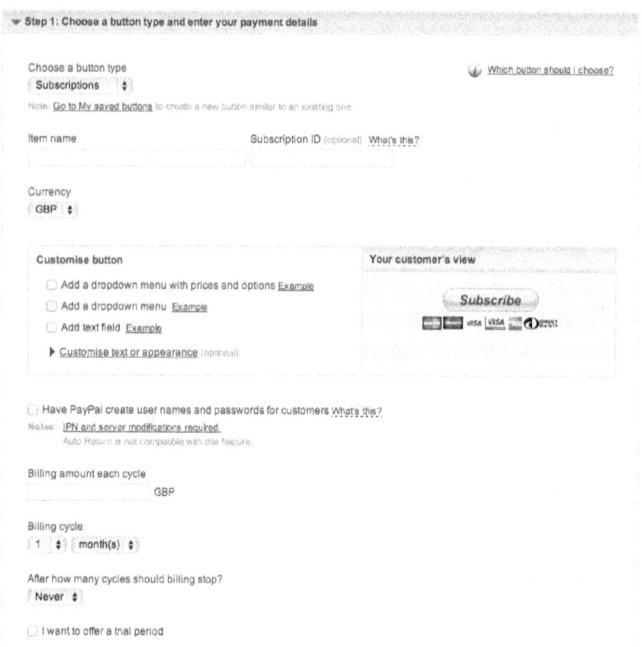

Now there are a few extra options to fill in. You'll need to complete the following:

Item Name: Give your subscription a unique name so you and your customer recognize what it's for.

Currency: Choose the currency you and your customers prefer.

Billing Amount Each Cycle: How much do you want your customer to be billed each time? Enter it here.

Billing Cycle: How often do you want your customers to be billed? You can choose whatever you want here - every month, every 1 week, every

1 year... the choice is yours.

After how many cycles should billing stop? If you know your eCourse ends after 12 monthly payments, select 12 in this dropdown. If you plan to continue the eCourse indefinitely, leave it selected on Never.

Trial Period: If you want to offer 1 week free, or 1 month at a reduced price, select the trial period check box and enter the details.

Now press Create Button.

Add your button code to your webpage

You just created customised HTML code for your button. The final step is to copy the code from this page and paste it into your website editor.

Copy the button code:

1. Click **Select Code**.
2. Right-click and copy the selected code.

If you're working with a website developer, you can paste the button code into an email and send it to your developer now.

Paste the button code in your website editor:

The code must be pasted in the "code" view, where you can view and edit HTML.

1. In your website editor or admin page, open the page where you want to add your button.
2. Look for an option to view or edit HTML.
3. Find the section of the page where you want your button to appear.
4. Right-click and paste your button code into the HTML.
5. Save and publish the page. (The preview function in your editor may not display the button code correctly.)
6. Test the button to make sure it links to a PayPal payment page.

Need more help? Click here for additional information.

And now you're presented with the code again, just as you were for the one time payment button above. Just follow the instructions PayPal gives for using your links. You can then link this into your

Aweber eCourse by using Aweber's PayPal app (see the separate tutorial).

Linking PayPal With Aweber Using the Aweber App

1) Load the PayPal App in Aweber

First, login to your Aweber account and then click **My Apps.**

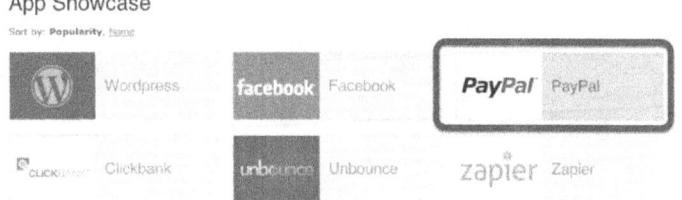

Next, scroll down and select the **PayPal** app.

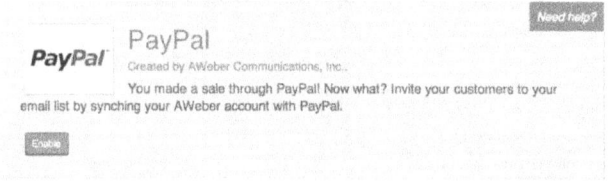

Click **Enable.**

2) Set Up the App in PayPal

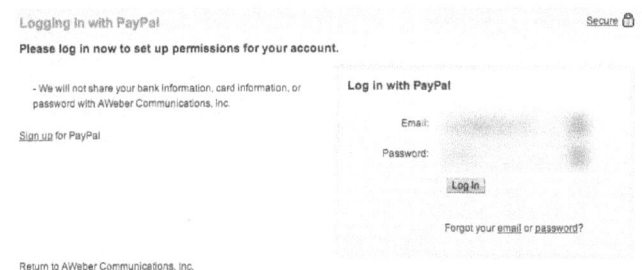

Now you'll be redirected to PayPal - login as normal with your mail seller account details.

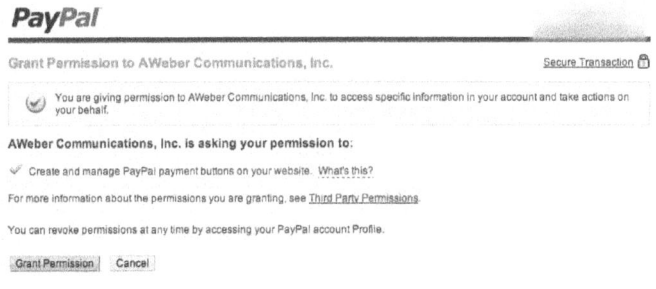

Click **Grant Permission**.

3) Follow the Aweber Setup Instructions

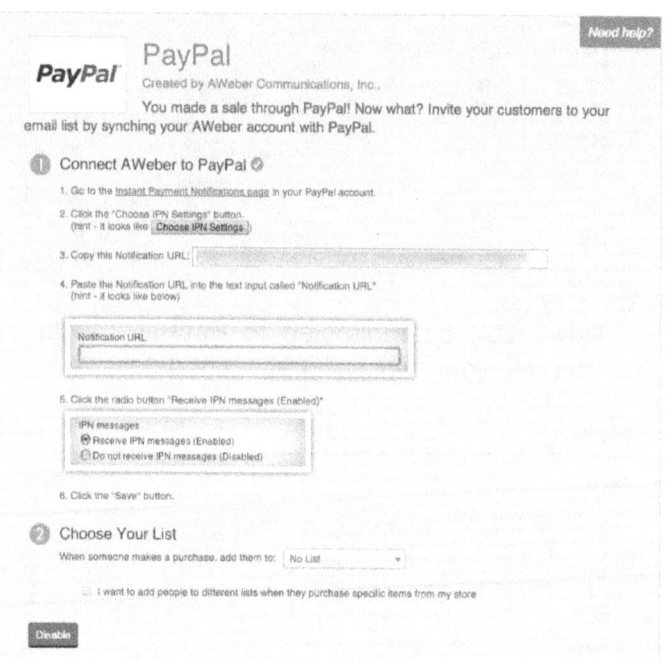

You'll now be redirected back to this page in Aweber. You'll also be sent an email with all the details in case you want to complete the steps later.

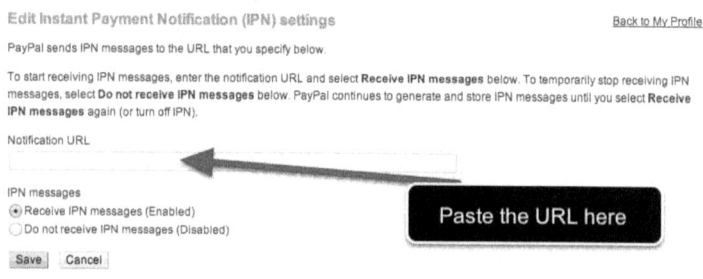

Simply go through the instructions on that page. First that means going to your Instant Payment Notifications page: https://www.paypal.com/us/cgi-bin/webscr?cmd=_profile-ipn-notify

Then pasting in the URL Aweber gave you onto that page, before clicking save.

4) Select Different Lists for Different Buy Buttons

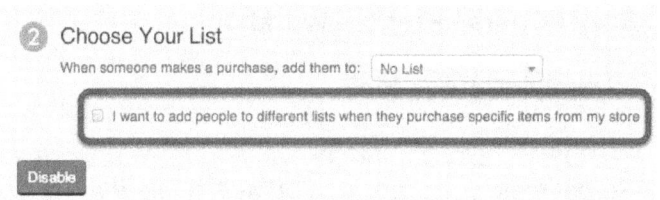

Now go back to the Aweber instructions page and have a look at Step 2. You'll see here that you can either add all your PayPal buyers to the same list, by choosing it from the dropdown menu. This is unsuitable if you sell more than one product via PayPal. This is why you'll probably want to check the box that says "I want to add people to different lists when they purchase specific items from my store"

If you haven't created your PayPal buttons yet, don't worry! Go back and follow that tutorial before coming back to the PayPal apps page and changing the setting here.

And if you haven't yet created your Aweber list, don't worry! Go back and follow that tutorial.

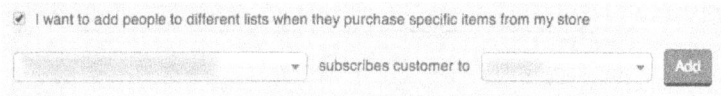

When you select the box to add people to different lists, you'll be shown a dropdown list of all the buttons you've created in PayPal, and all the lists you've created in Aweber. Simply match up the right button to the right eCourse list. You can add as many rules as you want, just click "Add" after each one! Now you're done!

Easy eCourse Profits - Workbook

1) My eCourse Ideas

Notes: Don't judge any of your ideas! Sometimes you can let yourself think they're not good enough, but just list them all here.

List 10 General eCourse Ideas:

_____

_____

_____

_____

_____

_____

_____

_____

_____

_____

_____

Finding It Hard? Try These Questions:

If you're not finding it easy to come up with good ideas on your own, use these questions to help.

List 5 Problems or Struggles Your Audience Has:

_____

_____

_____

_____

_____

Go to Forums In Your Niche/ Yahoo Answers.

Write Down 5 Questions You Found There:

_____

_____

_____

_____

_____

Visit Amazon.com and Find Top Books In Your Niche. Use the "Look Inside" Feature And List Some Chapter Titles Here:

These could later be broken down into step-by-step courses!

_____

_____

_____

_____

_____

2) eCourse Planning Sheet

Now, take one of the ideas you came up with in step 1. We're going to break it down into a full eCourse.

Main eCourse Topic:

_____

eCourse Delivery Frequency

Every week ☐   2-Weekly ☐ Monthly ☐   Other

_____

How Long Will The eCourse Last?

_____ days/ weeks/ months

How Many Steps Will You Need?

_____

For example, a 6 month eCourse, delivered once per week, will need 26 steps.

When Do You Plan to Launch Your eCourse?

Month   /   day   /   Year

Your Outline

Now break up your topic into the number of steps you need. Write each step here. This will form your outline.

_____

_____

_____

_____

_____

eCourse Steps Continued

_____

_____

_____

_____

_____

_____

_____

3) eCourse Setup Checklist

Once you've written your eCourse, it's time to set it up. Use this sheet to make sure everything's done.

Welcome Email Written?   ☐

First Email of eCourse Written?   ☐

PayPal Button Created?   ☐

Name of PayPal Button

_____

Aweber List Created?   ☐

Name of Aweber List

_____

PayPal Button & Aweber List Linked in Aweber

App ☐

Sales Page Created? ☐

Sent Email to Let Current Customers Know About
New List ☐

**Remember to keep writing your eCourse at
least one week in advance so that you never fall
behind with delivery!**

Congratulations on launching your eCourse!

*These are all the tools and links mentioned in
the training. There may be other services available,
but these are the ones we recommend.*

Core Tools

- **Aweber:**http://www.aweber.com/easy-
  email.htm?id=379016
- **Aweber Apps Page:**
  https://www.aweber.com/users/apps
- **PayPal:** http://www.paypal.com
- **PayPal Button Documentation:**

https://developer.paypal.com/webapps/developer/d
ocs/classic/paypal-payments-standard/integration-
guide/wp_standard_overview/

Brainstorming Resources

- **FreeMind:** http://freemind.sourceforge.net/

- **Yahoo Answers:** http://answers.yahoo.com/

- **Amazon.com Books:**
  http://www.amazon.com/books

Outsourcing

- **Upwork:** http://upwork.com/

- **Elance:** https://www.elance.com/

- **Constant Content:** https://www.constant-content.com/

- **All Custom Content:**
  http://www.allcustomcontent.com/

- **Text Broker:** http://www.textbroker.com/

Conclusion

There are lots of ways to make money from your knowledge. However, as you have learned, eCourses could be the perfect way to get started without getting stuck with the tech headaches!

Remember: there are no hard and fast rules for your eCourse. It could be quite short and last only 7 days, it could be a 6-month in depth video course, or it could be a yearlong series of short tips.

You need to go for whatever suits you, and whatever your market will find useful. And remember, you can always edit your eCourse in the future as you get more feedback from those who have completed it!

Whatever you do, don't get hung up on the little details. As long as you have knowledge to share, you can sell an eCourse!

So go and get brainstorming!

ABOUT THE AUTHOR

Chris Lutz is the founder and owner of
<u>S.P.A.R.T.A.</u> With more than a decade of
professional experience and a business owner, his
business now provides other business owners with
tools and resources to run more professional and
organized operations.
]
Chris owns and consults for other businesses in all
industries currently and is the author of several
other books –
The Entrepreneur Lifestyle
*Start, Operate, and Grow Your Personal Training
Business*
Metabolic Resistance Training
Maximum Fat Loss, Minimum Time
*Is Your Healthy Diet Making You Fat? Why You
Can't Seem to Lose Fat No Matter What You Do.*

His website, www.theentrepreneurlifestyle.com is a
celebration of the lifestyle of entrepreneurs and
teaches them how to go from struggle to success
with tools, eCourses, and other resources for
entrepreneurs.

Chris' other website, www.lutzlures.com is an
ecommerce site for the outdoor enthusiast and,
specifically kayak fishermen.